he Split History of the

JACOBITE REBELLIONS

THE HANOVERIAN PERSPECTIVE

BY CLAIRE THROP

CONTENT CONSULTANT:
Dr Linsey Hunter
Lecturer and Teaching Assistant at the University of the Highlands and Islands

raintree
a Capstone company — publishers for children

ABOUT THE AUTHOR:

Claire Throp grew up in High Wycombe, Buckinghamshire. She worked as an editor in publishing for 18 years before becoming an author. Claire has written books on all sorts of subjects, including history, science and geography, and now lives in Lincolnshire.

SOURCE NOTES:

The Jacobites' perspective

Page 4, line 4 *(p.22)*; page 14, line 8 *(p.15)*; page 15, line 2 *(p.51)*; page 17, line 2 *(p.159)*, line 6 *(p.7)*: *1715: The Great Jacobite Rebellion*, Daniel Szechi (Yale University Press, 2006)

Page 4, line 8: www.royal.gov.uk/HistoryoftheMonarchy/KingsandQueensoftheUnitedKingdom/TheStuarts/JamesII.aspx

Page 7, line 9 *(p.144)*; page 9, line 3 *(p.147)*; page 21, line 5 *(p.175)*; page 21, line 14 *(p.176)*; page 24, line 12 *(p.181)*; page 27, panel, line 10 *(pp. 166–167)*; page 28, line 17 *(p.199)*: *Battlefield Britain*, Peter and Dan Snow (BBC Books, 2004)

Page 11, line 7: *Ungrateful Daughters*, Maureen Waller (Hodder & Stoughton, 2002), page 367

Page 16, line 6: www.nationalarchives.gov.uk/education/resources/jacobite-1715/jacobites-earl-mar-sheriffmuir/

Page 18, line 5 *(p.40)*; page 21, line 16 *(p.45)*: *Sweet William or The Butcher?*, Jonathan Oates (Pen & Sword Military, 2008)

Page 22, line 4 *(p.35)*; page 22, line 21 *(p.41)*; page 23, line 7 *(p.41)*; page 25, line 3 *(p.45)*: *Culloden Guidebook*, Lyndsey Bowditch (The National Trust for Scotland, 2013)

Page 25, line 8: National Trust for Scotland, Resource Bank 53

Page 27, line 8: Culloden Visitor Centre, Resource Bank 10

Page 28, line 16: www.britannica.com/topic/Jacobite-British-history

Hanoverians' perspective

Page 5, illustration; page 6, photo; page 9, photo: www.nationalarchives.gov.uk/education/resources/jacobite-1715/stuart-family-tree/

Page 6, line 3 *(p.142)*; page 7, line 5 *(p.144)*; page 8, line 17 *(p.148)*; page 9, line 6 *(p.154)*; page 22, lines 3 and 8 *(p.176)*; page 23, lines 10 and 13 *(p.178)*; page 24, line 11 *(p.178)*: Snow

Page 8, line 5: http://portal.historic-scotland.gov.uk/designation/BTL32

Page 10, line 15: www.bbc.co.uk/history/scottishhistory/union/trails_union_glencoe.shtml

Page 15, line 19: Szechi, page 159

Page 15, line 22: www.nationalarchives.gov.uk/education/resources/jacobite-1715/lord-argyll/

Page 20, line 6 *(p.41)*; page 20, line 23 and page 21, line 5 *(p.42)*; page 21, lines 7 and 8 *(p.45)*: Oates

Page 25, line 6 (Resource Bank 54) and line 14 (Resource Banks 53–55): National Trust for Scotland

Contents

CHAPTER 1

THE SUCCESSION

In 1685, James II became king after the death of his brother, Charles II. As the grandson of James I of England and James VI of Scotland, from the House of Stuart, James ruled England (as James II), Scotland (as James VII) and Ireland. What caused much concern in Protestant England was that James was the first Catholic monarch in 130 years.

James II had turned to Catholicism late in life and had begun appointing Catholics to top jobs. He wanted to give Catholicism a more powerful role, allowing Catholics freedom to worship as they pleased, despite the fact that his kingdom was overwhelmingly Protestant.

Protestants became more and more worried about the likelihood of a return to Popery, a belief that the Catholic Church would try to take over the kingdom. There was also fear that the most powerful Catholic country in Europe, France, ruled by Louis XIV, would dominate England.

A NEW HEIR

In Protestant eyes, the situation worsened in 1688 when James's second wife, Mary of Modena, had a son, James Francis Edward Stuart. This meant that James II's Protestant daughter Mary was no longer first in line to the throne. Mary had married her cousin Prince William of Orange, from the Netherlands, in 1677. William was Protestant and had spent years fighting the French in the Netherlands.

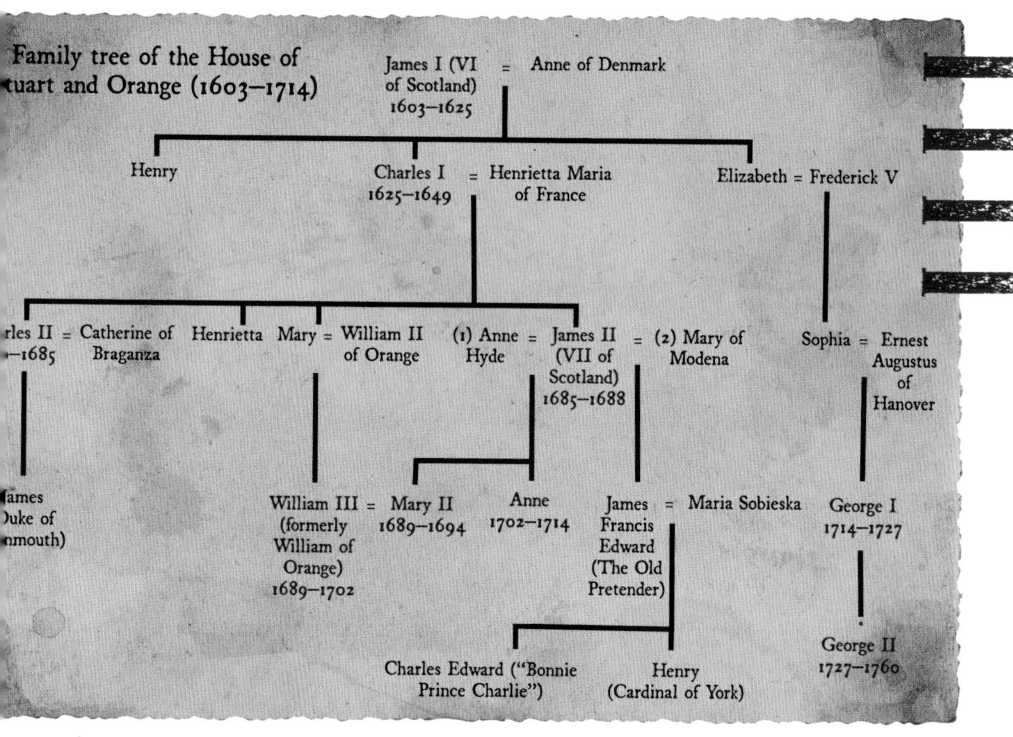

The Stuart family tree, including the reigns of the kings and queens

GLORIOUS REVOLUTION

In June 1688, six Protestant Members of Parliament (MPs) and one bishop asked William of Orange to come to England and help save it from James's Catholicism. William was happy to do so, not least because it would give him more power with which to fight the strongest Catholic European power, France. On 5 November, he landed in Devon with 10,000 men. Many English people supported William and when some of James II's supporters backed William instead, James fled to France. Officially, James II was assumed to have given up his crown, so Parliament asked William and Mary to rule jointly the kingdoms of England, Scotland and Ireland. While many people supported this move, there were others – mainly Catholics – in all three countries who were loyal to James. They became known as Jacobites.

William and Mary also accepted the Bill of Rights, which recognized Parliament's authority. The Bill stated that no monarch could rule without Parliament.

William III and Mary II

CHAPTER 2

THE JACOBITES RISE

John Graham, Viscount Dundee led the first Jacobite uprising. The fact that the Scottish Parliament supported William and Mary for the Scottish crown, not James II, angered Viscount Dundee. The arrival of James II and his French army in Ireland in March 1689 also inspired him to battle.

BATTLE OF KILLIECRANKIE

Clan chief Cameron of Lochiel led Dundee's Jacobite army, supported by a small force of Irish soldiers. The government army included Lowlanders (men from the south and east of Scotland), and English and Dutch troops under General Mackay. The two sides met at the Pass of Killiecrankie on 27 July 1689. The Jacobites took the government soldiers by surprise and many struggled to escape.

BATTLE OF DUNKELD

Viscount Dundee was injured in the battle and died. The government did not want the Jacobites to have time to regroup, so on 21 August, the two sides met again at Dunkeld. The government army consisted of 800 inexperienced men. They faced a Jacobite army of about 5,000 men. Vicious fighting took place. But just as the government army was close to losing, the Jacobites retreated. After this defeat, the Jacobite force faded.

IRELAND

Most of Ireland had welcomed James II in 1689, but he faced resistance from Protestants in the north. King William thwarted James's siege of Protestant Londonderry when he sent supply ships to break the blockade.

William also sent the Duke of Schomberg to end James's rebellion, but the duke failed in his mission. So in June 1690, William decided to take a huge force to Ireland to fight not only James, but indirectly also the man who backed James: King Louis XIV of France.

BATTLE OF THE BOYNE

The Battle of the Boyne took place on 1 July 1690. James had about 29,000 men, whereas King William had about 36,000. Most of James's men were camped south of the River Boyne, at Oldbridge, one of two main places to cross the river. William decided to keep most of his men north of the river at Oldbridge too, but he also sent a smaller group to cross at Rosnaree early in the morning.

Jacobite sentries mistakenly thought the whole of William's army was crossing at Rosnaree. So James marched his army to join the 800 men he had left to guard Rosnaree. But they arrived too late. James's men were outnumbered and defeated. Then James heard the terrible news that William's main force – 25,000 men – was now starting to fight at Oldbridge. James had left only 6,000 men there. Defeat meant the end of James's attempt to regain the throne. He returned to exile in France and William's conquest of England, Scotland and Ireland was complete.

William III's army defeated James II's army at the Battle of the Boyne, 1 July 1690.

GLENCOE MASSACRE

William saw Scotland and its clans as an irritation. In an attempt to keep the Highlands quiet, William offered the clans a pardon if they swore allegiance to William and Mary by 1 January 1692. However, many had sworn an oath to James II and it took a while for him to release them from that oath. Word finally got through just three days before the deadline.

Alasdair MacDonald, chief of the MacDonalds of Glencoe, set off to take the oath. On the way, the Campbells, an enemy clan, captured Alasdair MacDonald for one day. He then had to walk almost 100 kilometres (60 miles) because the oath had to be taken in front of a sheriff. But it was too late; the deadline had passed. The government's representative, Sir John Dalrymple, refused Alasdair MacDonald's oath. Dalrymple was a Protestant from the Scottish Lowlands who did not appreciate the Highlanders' way of life, particularly disliking the MacDonalds. He decided to finally destroy the MacDonald clan, declaring that they should be slaughtered: "Cut off root and branch".

In early February 1692, soldiers led by Captain Robert Campbell requested shelter in the homes of the MacDonalds because the nearby fort was full. The soldiers had been sent there deliberately. Twelve days later, on the morning of 13 February, the soldiers massacred the MacDonalds. Thirty-eight people were killed. The government had ordered the murder of the MacDonalds to keep the other clans in line.

The massacre caused outrage in Scotland. William ordered an enquiry into what had happened. The Scottish Parliament suggested it was murder. Dalrymple was eventually blamed and he resigned from his job. No other action was taken.

CHAPTER 3

IMPORTANT ACTS

In September 1701, James II died. James Francis Edward Stuart, James II's son, was recognized by French king Louis XIV as the rightful King of Scotland, England and Ireland, despite the fact that Louis XIV had no legal right to make this claim. Six months later, in March 1702, William died from an injury he got from falling off his horse. Mary II had died in 1694, so Anne, James II's youngest (Protestant) daughter, became queen.

ACT OF SETTLEMENT

The Act of Settlement in 1701 said that no Catholic, or anyone married to a Catholic, could be the English monarch. It established the order of succession: if William and Mary, and then Anne, had no heirs, the throne should pass to the Protestant Sophia of Hanover, granddaughter of James I. This meant that the royal house would change from the Stuart family to the Hanoverians.

ACT OF UNION

In May 1707, the Act of Union was passed, bringing England and Scotland together into one kingdom, with one Parliament based in London. The Act was supposed to remove the threat of Jacobitism, but it did the opposite. While the Jacobites stirred up trouble against the Union, the taxes that were added to Scottish goods to bring them in line with those taxed in England caused a great deal of discontent.

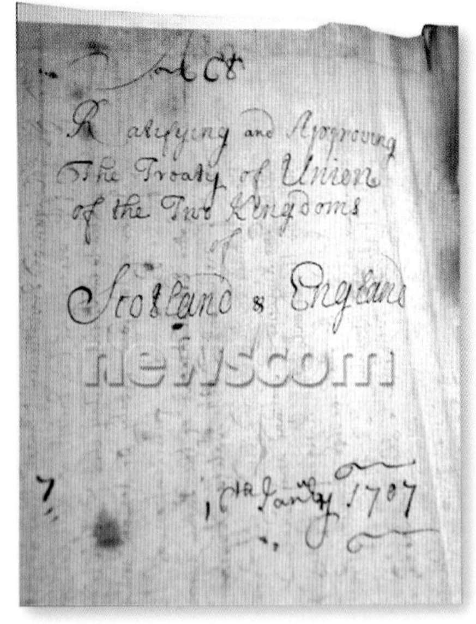

Act
Ratifying and Approving
The Treaty of Union
of the Two Kingdoms
of
Scotland & England
16th Janry 1707

The first page of the Act of Union treaty

1708 RISING

Taking advantage of this discontent, the French backed 19-year-old James Francis Edward Stuart, son of James II, in an attempt to invade Britain in January 1708. His ships had to battle gales in the North Sea before British warships forced them back. The rising failed.

A CHANGE OF MONARCH

Queen Anne died in August 1714. Sophia of Hanover had died in June, so the British throne now passed to her son, the Elector of Hanover, who became King George I. There were 50 Catholic royals who had stronger claims to the British throne but, as set out in the Act of Settlement, the Protestant George became king.

CHAPTER 4

THE 1715 REBELLION

The Jacobite Rebellion of 1715 arose because of a crisis in Britain: the change of royal house from the Stuarts to the Hanoverians and the Act of Union. The new king, George I, supported the Whigs' political party. George blamed the Tories for stirring up Scottish riots, and he wanted them out so that he could restart war with France. With the Whigs in power from 1714, the Tories were forced into supporting the Jacobite cause as a way to regain power.

King George I

TORIES AND WHIGS

The British Parliament was still largely dominated by English politicians. The two main groups in Parliament were the Tories and the Whigs. Whigamores were Scottish Presbyterians who rioted against the Church, so the name Whig suggested rebellion and refers to the group who, back in 1689, had wanted James II ousted from the throne. They believed in a balance of power between monarch and Parliament. Those who supported James and his belief in the absolute power of the monarch over Parliament were called Tories, an Irish term that meant "Catholic outlaw".

UNREST

While 1713 saw protests about the salt tax in Scotland, the Hanoverians faced opposition in England, too. Troops were sent out on the streets to try to calm things down. It was thought that the north of England was up to 25 per cent Catholic, so the government was constantly worried about uprisings there.

While Hanoverian troops in Scotland were generally veterans or inexperienced, the 1715 Rebellion in Scotland did not have any foreign influence or support. The 1713 Treaty of Utrecht, signed by Britain and France after years of war, banned the French from helping the Stuarts. Jacobites still hoping for secret help from Louis XIV were disappointed when he died on 1 September.

The Whigs certainly did not fear an uprising – they thought it would be madness for a rising with no outside support. However, many underestimated the strength of feeling that still existed against the Union.

THE EARL OF MAR

Scottish politician John Erskine, Earl of Mar, who had been dismissed as Secretary of State for Scotland when George I took the throne, turned to Jacobitism. He raised a standard to the Stuarts at Braemar, with the arms of Scotland on one side and "No Union" on the other. Those Scots unhappy with taxation and poverty flocked to him and he was soon in control of the north of Scotland, with command of 16,000 men.

BATTLE OF SHERIFFMUIR

On 13 November 1715, a Hanoverian army, led by the Duke of Argyll, and the Jacobites, led by the Earl of Mar, met at the Battle of Sheriffmuir near Stirling, Scotland. Argyll's men were heavily outnumbered. Chaos reigned during the battle, with one side chasing the other and vice versa. By evening, neither side wished to fight on, so the government troops headed back to Dunblane while the Jacobites returned to Perth. Argyll had lost almost 40 per cent of his men. The result was probably a draw, although both sides claimed victory. Afterwards, Argyll wrote to King George, "By the vast number of Rebells [Jacobites] we drove before us I could not … but judge it an entire Rout [victory]".

The rest of the 1715 Rebellion did not amount to much. Argyll was relieved as he thought the Hanoverians would have lost the country had the Jacobites risen again after Sheriffmuir. Another, smaller Jacobite army was defeated at Preston in northern England also on 13 November. The arrival of James Francis Edward Stuart in December did little to boost the Jacobites and soon the rebellion was over. James Francis Edward and the Earl of Mar fled to France.

The Earl Marischal and his Spanish army landed at Eilean Donan Castle, on the banks of Loch Duich, to join the Jacobite forces *(see page 17)**.*

CHAPTER 5

ANOTHER FAILED RISING

The 1715 uprising shocked the Hanoverians. As a result, a Disarming Act was passed in 1716. It banned Highlanders from carrying broadswords, muskets or other weapons in public. Soldiers' barracks were built in various parts of Scotland, too. This meant that men would be available far quicker were any further rebellions to break out. In fact, the next rebellion took place in 1719.

SPAIN AND THE JACOBITES

In April 1719, a small Spanish force under the Earl Marischal of Scotland landed at Eilean Donan Castle in the western Highlands of Scotland. The Catholic Spanish wanted revenge for the British destruction of Spanish ships off the coast of Sicily in August 1718. They used the Jacobite cause to pursue this revenge. A much larger force was supposed to invade south-west England, where there were still English Jacobites, but a storm destroyed many of the ships. The Royal Navy then forced the men camped at Eilean Donan Castle to abandon it, after which the navy destroyed the castle

The Jacobites, led by the Marquis of Tullibardine, and the Spanish were unable to agree on what to do next. On the way to Inverness, on 10 June 1719, General Joseph Wightman and the Hanoverians met the Jacobites at Glenshiel. Each side had roughly the same number of men, but Wightman used short guns called mortars, which set the heather alight, forcing the Highlanders to retreat. The Jacobites and the Spanish were defeated.

The Jacobite forces lost to the Hanoverians at the Battle of Glenshiel.

BARRACKS

Bernera Barracks at Glenelg, built in 1723, was the last of the four barracks to be placed in Scotland by the Hanoverians. Glenelg was an important place because it was close to the Isle of Skye, where there were many Stuart supporters, as well as the Jacobite Mackenzies to the north. A further Disarming Act in 1725 called for all weapons to be handed in to the government. The Hanoverians were trying to make sure that the Jacobites could not rise again.

CHAPTER 6

THE 1745 REBELLION

Jacobitism did not have much support in England from the 1720s. And while the Highland clans were ready to rise at any moment, for there to be any real possibility of defeating the Hanoverian army, they needed outside support. Foreign countries that were at peace with Britain had little reason to join forces with the Jacobites; this could provoke further wars.

The Hanoverians, now led by King George II, may have thought that the Jacobite threat had been dealt with, but Scottish disillusionment with the Union still existed, as did support for the Stuarts. The Tories in England were unable to gain any form of power in Parliament and Catholics were still being persecuted in Ireland. Jacobitism remained an important focus for these dissatisfied groups.

In May 1745, the French (with Jacobites fighting alongside them) defeated the British Army, led by the Duke of Cumberland, George II's son, at Fontenoy in Flanders (present-day Belgium). It seemed an ideal opportunity for the Jacobites to rise again.

THE ARRIVAL OF CHARLES

Charles Edward Stuart, who later became known as Bonnie Prince Charlie, arrived in Scotland in July 1745. At first, Charles struggled to persuade the Scottish Jacobites to join yet another fight for the crown. Politicians in England were happy to hear of his lack of support. Writer and Whig politician Horace Walpole wrote, "If the Boy [Charles] has no enemies in Scotland, at least he has openly very few friends." Although it took a while, Charles managed to gain enough supporters to form an army. Many Hanoverians were not worried, even after General Sir George Cope, who led the Hanoverian forces in Scotland, was unable to persuade any more men to fight for them while marching to battle.

However, the Duke of Newcastle, Secretary of State for the Southern Department in England, was concerned. He feared that the French would support the rebellion. The Hanoverian troops in Scotland were inexperienced – the best soldiers of the army were fighting under the Duke of Cumberland and others in Europe. Newcastle wrote to Cumberland twice, asking for the troops to return. But Cumberland did not think the situation serious enough to return to Britain with troops: "This cloud of the Pretender [Charles] will blow over". He sent 10 battalions (there were about 400–450 men in a battalion), stating that that should be enough. He said, "I hope Great Britain is not to be conquered by 3,000 rabble gather'd together in the mountains". The king and other members of the government agreed with him. Most people had little respect for the Jacobites at this point.

DUKE OF CUMBERLAND

William Augustus, Duke of Cumberland was George II's third son, born in London in 1721. He was the first Hanoverian to be British and speak English as his first language. William was well educated and was his father's favourite son. William joined the navy in 1740, then transferred to the army in 1742.

William Augustus, Duke of Cumberland

PANIC

The Jacobites, led by Bonnie Prince Charlie, easily took Edinburgh in September 1745 and followed this up with a win at the Battle of Prestonpans. Hanoverian forces fled and many were killed or captured. Andrew Henderson, Scottish schoolmaster and historian, wrote at the time, "The Infantry in the first line were miserably massacred by the Rebels."

These losses caused panic in England: "This defeat has frightened everybody," wrote Horace Walpole. Newcastle wrote: "You will also see that we have for the present lost one kingdom." The blow of losing Scotland was softened slightly when Dutch and Swiss troops, who had been fighting with the Hanoverians in Europe, arrived in Britain to help.

Parliament also finally recalled many more of the soldiers fighting abroad, including the Duke of Cumberland, in order to send 10,000 men to the north to fight the Jacobites.

This illustration shows the defeated General Sir John Cope racing away from the Battle of Prestonpans.

JACOBITES IN ENGLAND

Meanwhile, the Jacobites invaded England. Carlisle, Preston and Manchester fell easily to the Jacobites. The Hanoverian army did not know where the Jacobites were aiming for: London, Wales or Bristol. The Jacobites tricked the Hanoverians into thinking they would face them in Staffordshire, but they were, in fact, on their way to London. They reached Derby by 4 December.

While they tried to work out what to do next, the Jacobites met a wealthy sympathizer called Dudley Bradstreet. He told them that

Hanoverian troops blocked the way to London at Northampton. After much discussion, the Jacobites reluctantly turned back towards Scotland. What they did not know was that Bradstreet was a government spy – there was no army at Northampton.

Things were going badly for the government in London. They were having money problems. Neither Wade's nor Cumberland's armies would be in a position to help defend the city – even the king was readying himself to take up arms. They had heard that the French were about to invade, too. In fact, the French were ready to set sail on 20 December. With London in a state of panic and the French due to arrive, were the Jacobites to have continued their march southwards, they may well have been able to take the city.

SCOTLAND

The Jacobite forces had marched rapidly back towards Scotland. They attempted to storm Stirling, but their siege of the castle failed. In January 1746, however, they fought successfully at the Battle of Falkirk. The Hanoverian army, under General Henry Hawley, was now more familiar with, and therefore better able to deal with, Highland battle tactics. But some soldiers still panicked and fled. The Jacobite win came partly because Hawley had underestimated them, despite the fact that the Jacobites had won every battle against the Hanoverians so far. However, the Jacobites made a mistake in allowing most of the Hanoverian troops to retreat to Edinburgh.

TRAINING AND RECRUITMENT

On reaching Edinburgh on 30 January 1746, the Duke of Cumberland set to work training his men (known as the Redcoats because of the colour of coats they wore). His aim was to teach them how to resist the Highland charge and how to use their bayonets efficiently. Instead of the soldiers pushing their bayonets directly in front of them, they were trained to thrust the weapon into the right-hand side of the enemy Jacobite soldiers. The Jacobite facing them would probably have his arm raised, ready to use his sword, making it easier for a Hanoverian soldier to use his bayonet to stab a Jacobite's side.

The training sessions boosted morale and improved levels of trust among all the men. Cumberland also made sure that men who had run away at the Battle of Falkirk were hanged as a warning to others who might think of deserting the battlefield.

Cumberland decided to wait out the winter and eventually marched his Hanoverian army to Aberdeen. Once they had arrived in the city, they gathered supplies of food and weapons. They were now rested and well fed, in contrast to the Jacobites, who had no money and therefore little food. The Jacobites had no choice but to stay in Inverness because that's where their small reserves of food were.

CHAPTER 7

BATTLE OF CULLODEN

The Battle of Culloden was the last battle to be fought on British soil. It was over very quickly. "They [the Jacobites] choosed that Bogie [boggy] Moor to fight in by Reason they thought we could not bring up our Cannon through it, but, thank God, they were all mistaken," wrote Edward Linn, a Hanoverian soldier, to his wife.

At about 12.30 p.m. on 16 April 1746, the Jacobites fired the first shot, but then came under heavy fire from the better-armed government soldiers. Five minutes later, the Jacobite charge began. But they found it hard to charge over the boggy ground. Hand-to-hand fighting took place, with the Hanoverians using the Duke of Cumberland's specialist training to fight with bayonets. Over 1,000 Jacobites died. "I never saw a Small field thicker of Dead," wrote Linn. By 12.55, the Hanoverians surrounded the Jacobites. At 1 p.m., the Jacobites were in full retreat and Cumberland ordered the cavalry to pursue them from the field.

This painting shows the two armies lined up in formation during the Battle of Culloden.

AFTER THE BATTLE

The Duke of Cumberland's army of about 9,000 men had met the 5,000 Jacobites and won with ease. The Jacobites had tried to stage a surprise attack on the Hanoverians the night before, but without success. They were tired, weak and hungry, and they were no match for the disciplined Hanoverian soldiers.

Cumberland offered amnesty (an official pardon) to any Jacobites who surrendered, but some Highlanders continued to fight. This led to brutal raids: many were killed, buildings were burned and cattle and land were lost.

"BUTCHER" OR "DEAR BILL"?

Opinion on the Duke of Cumberland was divided. Those in favour of the Hanoverians called him "our dear Bill" or Sweet William; the Jacobites called him "the Butcher". He wrote "No Quarter", meaning no mercy, on the back of the nine of diamonds in a pack of cards (now known as the "curse of Scotland"). This was an order to kill any remaining Jacobite soldiers on sight, including the wounded ones.

But Cumberland did not do anything out of the ordinary for the time. Victors often pursued losers from the field. His amnesty had also been ignored. He had offered amnesty to those who surrendered, but when it was clear that was not going to happen, he gave the order to kill all Jacobites.

While still in Scotland, Cumberland emptied the jails of those imprisoned by Jacobite supporters and replaced them with Jacobite captives. Many prisoners were moved south to stand trial, while executions took place across England. In total, 120 Jacobite soldiers were executed, 936 men were transported to British colonies and a further 222 were banished. Hundreds were eventually released under the Act of Indemnity in 1747. All high-ranking Jacobites officers were executed on Tower Hill, London.

CHAPTER 8

JACOBITE THREAT DESTROYED

The 1745 Rebellion had come as a shock to the Hanoverians. There was a concern about the ease with which the Jacobites had won so many battles against the supposedly more experienced and more professional government troops. London came close to being lost at one stage and, had the Jacobites managed to get control of the capital city, it would have been a major victory for them, particularly with the French ready to invade.

The Jacobites were treated harshly after the Battle of Culloden because the Hanoverians didn't want them to be able to rally again. The government also had the threat of France to worry about, so they needed the threat of Jacobitism to be removed once and for all. It was time to break the Highland

THE ACT OF PROSCRIPTION

In order to break up the clan system entirely, the government passed a number of Acts in 1746 and 1747, including the Act of Proscription. These banned Highlanders from carrying weapons such as dirks (daggers) and muskets, and forbade the wearing of tartan. The Crown took all clan chief legal powers, which angered those clans who had fought for the Hanoverians. Jacobite estates were seized. The punishments were more severe than those suggested for the 1716 Disarming Act. Culloden spelled the end of Jacobitism.

WHAT HAPPENED TO THE STUARTS?

After Culloden, Jacobite supporters helped Charles Edward Stuart to hide out in the Western Isles of Scotland for about five months. He finally left Scotland on a ship bound for France in September 1746. Charles died in Rome, Italy, in 1789. One remaining Stuart – Henry – was a bishop in Italy. Jacobites knew him as King Henry IX after the death of Charles. He died in 1807.

The Hanoverians continued to rule Britain until 1901 and the death of Queen Victoria. To the present day, England, Scotland, Wales and Northern Ireland are mainly Protestant countries. Ireland is still largely Catholic.

Medals were made to commemorate the Hanoverian victory over the Jacobites.

INDEX

A PERSPECTIVES FLIP BOOK

The Split History of the JACOBITE REBELLIONS

THE JACOBITE PERSPECTIVE

BY CLAIRE THROP

CONTENT CONSULTANT:
Dr Linsey Hunter
Lecturer and Teaching Assistant at the University of the Highlands and Islands

Raintree is an imprint of Capstone Global Library Limited, a company incorporated in England and Wales having its registered office at 264 Banbury Road, Oxford, OX2 7DY – Registered company number: 6695582

www.raintree.co.uk
myorders@raintree.co.uk

Edited by Helen Cox Cannons
Designed by Philippa Jenkins
Original illustrations © Capstone Global Library Ltd 2016
Picture research by Kelly Garvin
Production by Victoria Fitzgerald
Originated by Capstone Global Library Ltd
Printed and bound in China

ISBN 978 1 4747 2716 7 (hardback)
20 19 18 17 16
10 9 8 7 6 5 4 3 2 1

ISBN 978 1 4747 2717 4 (paperback)
21 20 19 18 17
10 9 8 7 6 5 4 3 2 1

ACKNOWLEDGEMENTS

We would like to thank the following for permission to reproduce photographs:
Jacobite Perspective: Alamy Images: Chronicle, 23, GL Archive, cover (bottom), Pictorial Press, 15; Bridgeman Images/The Story of Scotland: Such an Odd Union, Escott, Dan (1928-87)/Private Collection/Look and Learn, 27 (left); Getty Images: Culture Club, 20, Mansell/The LIFE Picture Collection, 26; Mary Evans Picture Library: cover (top), Douglas McCarthy, 29; Newscom: Album/E.Viader/Prisma, 16, Design Pics, 8, Mondadori Portfolio via Getty Images, 19, Patrick Dieudonne/Robert Harding, 10, Sotheby's/akg-images, 14; Oxford Designers and Illustrators, 5, 25; Superstock: Universal Images Group, 6; The Image Works/The Board of Trustees of the Armouries/Heritage-Images, 27 (right).
Hanoverian Perspective: Alamy: Alan King engraving, 18, Chronicle, 22, GL Archive, cover (top), Timewatch Images, 29; Capstone Press/Philippa Jenkins, 5, Getty Images, Hulton Archive, 6, 21, Mary Evans Picture Library, cover (bottom), Newscom: akg-images, 13, James Fraser/REX, 12, Moreno, J./picture alliance/Arco Images G, 16, World History Archive, 9, 26, Shutterstock: designelements, 6, Marc Dietrich, 13.

We would like to thank Dr Linsey Hunter for her invaluable help in the preparation of this book.

Contents

SHARED RESOURCES

CHAPTER 1

CLANS AND MONARCHS

The Highlands and islands of Scotland include the west and north-west of Scotland. One of the features of the Highlands in the late 17th and early 18th centuries was that they consisted of clans of about 5,000–6,000 people.

KINGS AND QUEENS

In 1685, King Charles II died. His brother James, as the grandson of James I of England and VI of Scotland, from the House of Stuart, became King James II of England and Ireland and James VII of Scotland. James had become a Catholic in 1669 and married Mary of Modena, also a Catholic, in 1673. In June 1688, they had a son, James Francis Edward Stuart. He was born a month earlier than expected, which led to rumours that the baby was not Mary's. Some Protestants believed that the baby was smuggled in to ensure that James II had a Catholic heir. Whatever the truth, Protestants were worried. Catholics were being given top jobs in the army and government. James wanted to allow Catholics freedom of worship. But this ended up alienating the Protestants in the population.

THE CLAN SYSTEM

The clan system emerged in the Highlands of Scotland by at least the 11th century. The Gaelic word *clann* means "children", or "descendants", but this does not mean that every member of a clan was part of the same family. However, loyalty between clan members was strong: they often put clan before country. Powerful chiefs ran clans for the benefit of all clan members.

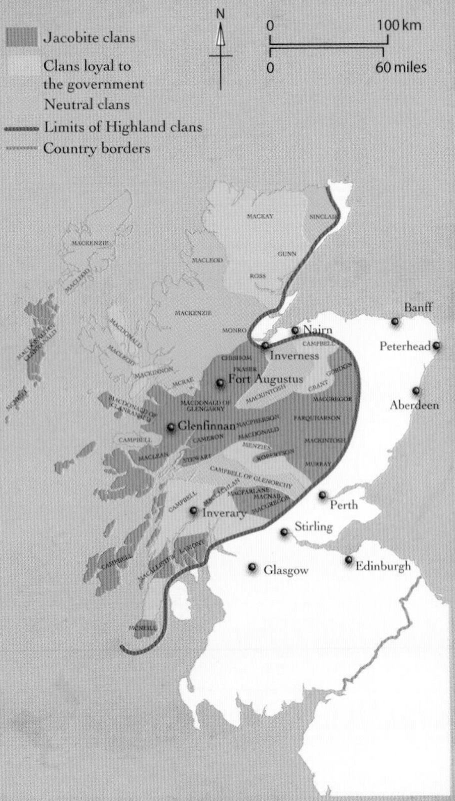

This map shows the whereabouts of the Scottish clans during the late 17th and early 18th centuries.

Mary, James's Protestant daughter from his first marriage, was no longer heir to the throne after the birth of James Francis Edward, since males were first in line before females. Mary had married her cousin, who was also James II's nephew, William of Orange, in 1677. He too was Protestant and was dedicated to fighting Catholic France, whose king was Louis XIV.

GLORIOUS REVOLUTION

William had already been thinking about invading England, so he was happy to receive an invitation from the English Parliament in 1688 to come to England and try to stop James II leading the country towards Catholicism.

William quickly gained military support. Soon afterwards, James escaped to France. Parliament then offered the throne to William and Mary to rule jointly, and they accepted. They also accepted the Bill of Rights, which said that no monarch would ever be able to rule without Parliament again. Parliament then happily gave William money to fight France. A defeat for France would be bad news for James II; France's king, Louis XIV, was James's main ally.

King James II of England was also James VII of Scotland.

CHAPTER 2

EARLY RISINGS

In early 1689, the Scottish Parliament decided to support the Protestant William and Mary rather than James II. Some Scots, including John Graham, Viscount Dundee, were unhappy with this decision. They declared in favour of James. Supporters of James became known as Jacobites, which comes from the Latin *Jacobus*, meaning "James".

While he was in France, James had been organizing an invasion. He arrived in Ireland on 12 March 1689 with 2,000 men provided by Louis XIV of France. James had no interest in Ireland itself: he simply wanted to use its Catholic soldiers as a means of regaining his throne. Apart from a number of Protestants in the north, Ireland was mainly Catholic and many welcomed James enthusiastically. The Irish Parliament also welcomed James, and together they issued an Act for Liberty of Conscience. This Act granted religious freedom to all Roman Catholics and Protestants in Ireland.

BATTLE OF KILLIECRANKIE

John Graham, Viscount Dundee

April 1689 saw the start of armed protest against the government – the first Jacobite uprising in Scotland. The Pass of Killiecrankie was part of a north–south route through the Highlands.

It was important to each side – the Jacobites and the government – to have control of the route. On 27 July 1689, the Jacobites, led by Viscount Dundee, fought government forces at the Battle of Killiecrankie. The battle was short. The Jacobites were positioned on a hill and smashed into the government soldiers, who soon fled the battleground. However, the Jacobites lost their leader and about a third of their men. Defeat at the Battle of Dunkeld in August, despite vastly outnumbering the government army, meant the end of the first Jacobite uprising.

BATTLE OF THE BOYNE

William had ordered the Duke of Schomberg to deal with James, but the elderly duke failed in his mission, so William sailed to Ireland himself in June 1690. On 1 July, the two sides met at the River Boyne

north of Dublin. There were two crossings: one at Oldbridge and one at Rosnaree. James placed most of his troops at Oldbridge and left 800 men at Rosnaree.

Later, James was mistakenly led to believe that all William's men were crossing at Rosnaree. James marched two-thirds of his army to join the rest at Rosnaree, leaving one-third at Oldbridge. But they arrived too late. Then he discovered that the larger part of William's army was still at Oldbridge. James's men there had no chance. William's victory forced James back into exile in France.

GLENCOE MASSACRE

In August 1691, clan chiefs were told that they would be pardoned for their part in Jacobite uprisings if they swore allegiance to King William and Queen Mary by 1 January 1692. However, many clans had sworn an oath to James II, who was in France. Getting permission from James to be released from the old oath took time – not least because James still thought he might be able to regain his throne. Eventually, though, he officially released the clans. By the time the news reached the Highlands, though, only three days remained until the deadline.

Alasdair MacDonald was chief of the MacDonald clan of Glencoe. He set out to take the oath with plenty of time left before the deadline, but faced a number of problems on the way, including a rival clan, the Campbells, capturing him for a day. The government's representative, Sir John Dalrymple, refused to accept the oath because MacDonald took it several days late. He decided to make an example of the MacDonald clan.

Usually, Highland culture was to be welcoming to other clans when they were in need, even if they had recently been fighting. In early February, when soldiers, including some Campbells, claimed to have nowhere to stay, the MacDonalds gave them shelter in their homes. What the MacDonalds didn't know was that the soldiers had been sent there on purpose.

On 13 February, Captain Robert Campbell gave his soldiers orders from the government to kill the MacDonalds. It is thought that some of the soldiers warned the MacDonalds because they did not agree with the order to kill. Even so, 38 people died. Those who managed to escape had to face the cold Scottish winter. Many perished. The massacre caused outrage in Scotland, particularly when the enquiry held afterwards did little to help calm the situation. Dalrymple resigned but he received no other punishment.

The Glencoe Massacre happened at these rugged mountains at Glencoe in Argyll.

CHAPTER 3

IN BETWEEN RISINGS

In September 1701, James II died. Although he had no power to do so, France's Louis XIV declared James Francis Edward Stuart, James's son, the rightful King of England, Scotland and Ireland. This enraged William and the people of England. However, in March 1702, William died from an injury he got falling off his horse when it tripped over a molehill. This caused Jacobites to raise a toast to the mole as the "little gentleman in black velvet". Mary II had died in 1694, so that left her sister Anne, also Protestant, who became queen.

ACT OF SETTLEMENT

England had been mainly Protestant since the late 16th century. The 1701 Act of Settlement stated that no Catholic, or anyone married to a Catholic, could become King or Queen of England. If William and Mary, and then Anne, had no surviving children, the throne should pass to the House of Hanover. Sophia of Hanover was the Protestant granddaughter of Stuart king James I (reigned 1603–1625).

ACT OF UNION

The Act of Union was created to combine England and Scotland into one kingdom, with its parliament in London. The English Parliament wanted to prevent the Catholic Stuarts from retaking the Scottish throne when Queen Anne died. They thought it might lead to a French-backed invasion to regain the English throne too. They needed a British crown that would pass straight to the Protestant House of Hanover.

When part of the Act was made public in October 1706, there were protests outside the Scottish Parliament building. In May 1707, the Act of Union was passed. While the Union was supposed to bring the two countries together, it actually caused some Scots to turn to Jacobitism. They thought that if James Francis Edward Stuart became king, he would separate the two countries again.

1708 RISING

It seemed like a good time for a Jacobite invasion. In January 1708, James Francis Edward Stuart tried to invade Britain in ships provided by the French king. But when James arrived at the Firth of Forth near Edinburgh after bad weather, the Royal Navy was waiting and chased the ships off.

THE HOUSE OF HANOVER

Queen Anne died in August 1714. She had no surviving children, so the throne was passed to the German House of Hanover. Sophia of Hanover had died a couple of months before Anne, so her son George was heir. He became King George I, and was crowned in October 1714.

CHAPTER 4

THE 1715 REBELLION

People had different reasons for turning to Jacobitism. Those Jacobites living in England and Wales wanted something different from those in Ireland and Scotland. For the Irish and Scots, religion (Catholicism) played a major role in their decision to fight against the Hanoverians. There were some English Jacobites fighting for their religion, too.

Many Scottish people wanted to return to a separation of Scotland and England. They had been promised economic benefits as a result of the 1707 Act of Union, but these had not yet happened. Also, the Scots now had more taxes to pay. Loyalty to the Stuarts was another factor for the Scots: the Stuarts had ruled Scotland since 1371. They were dedicated to returning the Stuart family and their line of heirs to the thrones of England, Scotland and Ireland.

THE OLD PRETENDER

James Francis Edward Stuart (nicknamed the Old Pretender) was born in 1688. He was the only son of James II and Mary of Modena. He had been sent abroad with his mother while his father tried to save his throne in late 1688. Young James had grown up at the French court and had fought in wars in Europe. In 1714, he refused to give up his Catholicism so he could become heir to the British throne.

James Francis Edward Stuart (The Old Pretender)

EARL OF MAR

John Erskine, Earl of Mar, had been Queen Anne's Secretary of State for Scotland, but he was dismissed when George I came to the throne in 1714. As a result, he turned to Jacobitism.

There were protests against taxes in Scotland in 1713. Mar used these to help gather support. In August 1715, he arrived in Scotland and declared that Parliament wanted to "lay unsupportable taxes upon the nation" and that the nation would soon "sink under such burdens [loads]". Unsurprisingly, his words encouraged the people to rise up.

Mar proclaimed James Francis Edward Stuart king of Great Britain in September 1715 at Braemar, Scotland. He raised a standard to the Stuarts, with the arms of Scotland on one side and "No Union" on the other. Mar had managed to raise 16,000 men, many of whom came from Highland clans and north-east Scotland.

John Erskine, Earl of Mar raising a standard in support of the Stuarts.

ENGLISH JACOBITES

Some people in England were unhappy at the idea of a foreign monarch, so there was a lot of support for the Jacobites in south-west England. However, when the king made it clear that he knew about French invasion plans, the Jacobites there went into hiding.

After failing to take the city of Newcastle, another group of English Jacobites in the north-east of England met up with Scottish Jacobites at the Scottish border. Unfortunately, they couldn't decide what to do next. The English wanted the Scots to march with them into England, but the Scots wanted to join the Earl of Mar in Perth.

BATTLE OF SHERIFFMUIR

Finally, Mar decided the time was right to fight. At the Battle of Sheriffmuir, the Jacobites had over 7,000 men, whereas the Duke of Argyll was in command of about 3,000 Hanoverian soldiers. The battle was chaotic and the result probably a draw, although both sides claimed victory. After the battle, the Earl of Mar wrote to the Governor of Perth that the Jacobites "Carry'd the day entirely".

ROB ROY

Robert MacGregor was born in 1671 in Stirlingshire. Along with his father, Donald, he fought for the Stuarts in the Battle of Killiecrankie in 1689. After his cattle-dealing business failed, he lived a life of cattle stealing and blackmail. He also played a part in the 1715 Rebellion, leading the MacGregors against the Hanoverians. He often signed his name Rob Roy (Red Rob) because he had red hair.

Robert "Rob Roy" MacGregor

The Jacobites lost around 17 per cent of their men at the Battle of Sheriffmuir. This was hundreds of men, but the survivors should have been able to continue fighting. Several Jacobite groups, including the troops led by Rob Roy, had not even had the chance to join the battle. However, the Earl of Mar was not a decisive leader and after the battle there were many desertions. This was partly because men who had fought believed they could then return home with the spoils.

Meanwhile, the Jacobites in northern England had marched south to Preston. Gradually, Hanoverian forces had surrounded them until surrender was unavoidable.

James Francis Edward Stuart didn't arrive in Scotland until it was too late, in December. He stayed with the Jacobite troops until February but was unable to inspire the men to fight on. He returned to Italy. The rebellion had collapsed.

THE LITTLE RISING

Another Catholic country helped the Jacobites in 1719: Spain. What became known as the "Little Rising" was set in motion at least in part because the Spanish were angry that the British had destroyed their ships the previous year. Unfortunately, bad weather held up the main part of Spain's invasion force, which planned to land in south-west England, so only a small number of Spaniards made it to Scotland. After the navy managed to chase the Spanish and Jacobites from Eilean Donan Castle in the western Highlands, General Wightman of the Hanoverian army met them at Glenshiel in June. After several hours fighting, Wightman and his army forced the Jacobites to retreat.

CHAPTER 5 1745

While war in Europe distracted Britain, it was the ideal time for Charles, son of James Francis Edward Stuart, to invade. Charles and the French army's attempt to land in Britain in early 1744, when Britain was involved in the Austrian War of Succession, was frustrated by bad weather. But Charles didn't give up.

GATHERING SUPPORT

In July 1745, Charles finally landed in Scotland. He had left France with 700 men, but lost the majority when a British navy ship fired on them. However, he was determined that he would regain the throne his family deserved by right.

At first, Charles found it difficult to build support. Highlanders were not impressed when they realized there was no immediate backing from the French. Charles told the Highlanders that the French had promised to invade, and that the English Jacobites would join them if he first got control of Scotland and then invaded England. This helped to persuade some Scottish Jacobites to follow Charles.

However, some clans, such as the Campbells and the Sutherlands, were doing well under the Hanoverians. They also remembered the 1715 Rebellion. They wanted to avoid the messiness of rebellion and government punishments.

Finally, on 19 August, Charles raised his standard at Glenfinnan in the Highlands, and waited with 400 men. Eventually, Cameron of Lochiel arrived with another 800 men.

BONNIE PRINCE CHARLIE

Charles Edward Stuart was known as Bonnie Prince Charlie. As the son of the "Old Pretender", he was also known as the "Young Pretender". Charles was handsome and charming, but not very Scottish. He was born in 1720 in Rome, Italy, and he mainly spoke Italian and French. Charles was brought up a Catholic. He learned how to fight at a young age. He was determined to be a good Jacobite leader, so he wore kilts and marched on foot with his men.

Charles Edward Stuart (Bonnie Prince Charlie)

CHARLES ON THE MARCH

Many of Charles's men had been forced into joining – the chief of a clan could beat them or burn down their houses to get them to follow him. But Charles now had an army. They marched on Edinburgh in September. They successfully avoided General Sir George Cope, who led the Hanoverian forces in Scotland. His 1,400 men were slow-moving and ended up sailing from Aberdeen to get to Edinburgh. They arrived too late: the Jacobites had easily taken the city. The Hanoverian forces marched from the port of Dunbar to Prestonpans, south of Edinburgh.

Bonnie Prince Charlie and his army marched through Edinburgh.

BATTLE OF PRESTONPANS

On 20 September 1745, a battle took place at Prestonpans between the Jacobites and the Hanoverians. Each army had about 2,500 men. The Highland charge was successful. The Hanoverian army fled, but many were cut down as they tried to escape. About 300 Hanoverians were killed compared with only 25 Jacobites. The Hanoverians finally began to realize that this Jacobite rebellion was a serious threat.

ARGUMENTS

Charles, feeling confident, now wanted to invade England. He did not want to rule Scotland alone – he wanted England as well. An experienced Jacobite general, Lord George Murray, was in his way. He clashed with Charles, arguing that they were better off securing Scotland first. Murray knew going to England was a mistake, but Charles argued that the English Jacobites would join them. At a Council of War meeting at Holyroodhouse in Edinburgh, the army leaders voted. Charles won the vote by one.

INTO ENGLAND

The Jacobites marched into England with great speed, reaching Carlisle in a couple of weeks. Around 1,000 men had deserted, however; many Scots did not want to leave the relative safety of their home country, fearful of how they would be received in England. While Charles's army had met little resistance on his march into England, it had attracted very few recruits.

THE COUNCIL OF WAR

At the Council of War set up to decide what to do next, the Jacobite leaders discussed four options: returning to Scotland; marching against the Hanoverian army under the command of Wade; staying in Carlisle and hoping to attract more recruits; or continuing to march towards London. Charles wanted to go to London, but his officers wanted to return to Scotland. Charles won the vote again.

TRICKED

By 4 December, the Jacobites had got as far south as Derby before realizing that there was very little English support for them. There was no definite news of the French lending support either. When the Jacobites heard that a Hanoverian army was camped at Northampton and blocking their route to London, they decided that their only option was to return to Scotland. But the army at Northampton did not exist – a government spy had tricked them. The French also postponed their planned invasion, and finally cancelled it altogether after the Jacobites retreated to Scotland.

SUCCESS DESPITE RETREAT

The city of Glasgow was happy and successful under the Hanoverians. Its people wanted nothing to do with the Jacobites. On their return, the Jacobites had to force the people of Glasgow to provide supplies. They then set off for Stirling. They attempted – unsuccessfully – to lay siege to Stirling Castle. More men joined them from the north of Scotland: there were now 8,000–9000 men in the Jacobite army.

Some supplies and money also still came in from the French, entering through the ports in the north-east of Scotland.

The Jacobites claimed yet another victory over the Hanoverians at Falkirk on 17 January 1746, but they did not build upon their success. They allowed the Hanoverian commander, Lieutenant General Henry Hawley, to retreat to Edinburgh. The government army had lost 350 men with 300 more either injured or captured. The Jacobites moved further north to Inverness and remained there for two months.

This painting shows Bonnie Prince Charlie taking prisoners from the Battle of Falkirk to Doune Castle, near Stirling.

CHAPTER 6

BATTLE OF CULLODEN

When Charles heard that the Duke of Cumberland had reached Nairn about 19 kilometres (12 miles) away, a Council of War was called. The council decided to surprise the duke and his men with a dawn attack. It was the duke's birthday, and the Jacobites hoped that the Hanoverians had been celebrating and would be unprepared for a fight.

Two columns of men, one led by Charles and one by Lord George Murray, marched towards Nairn on the evening of 15 April 1746. The rough ground made marching difficult and the men had barely eaten all day. They got as far as 6.5 kilometres (4 miles) from Nairn when Murray decided to turn back, as they were losing light. Charles was enraged and shouted "I am betrayed!" In fact, some men did make it into position in time, but without Murray's men, they too had to retreat. As Cumberland's men were being woken in preparation for battle, many of the hungry, tired Jacobites were already on the road to Inverness.

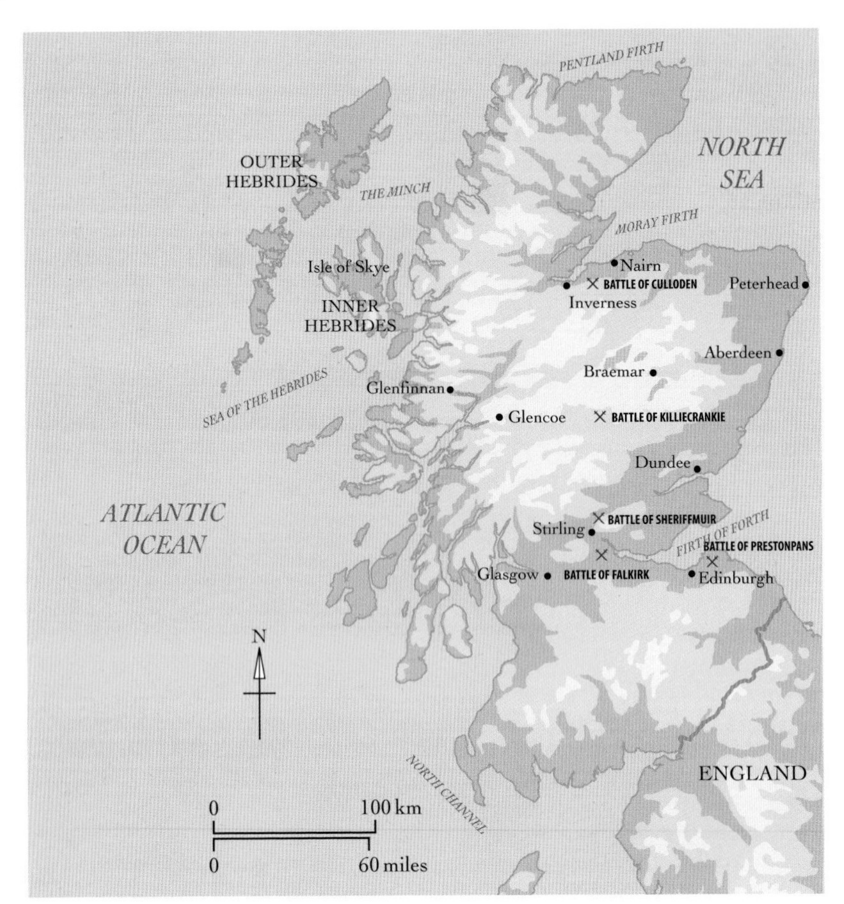

This map shows the location of the Battle of Culloden and other key battles mentioned in this book.

BATTLEGROUND

The arguments over the battleground may have contributed to the Jacobites' defeat. Lord George Murray wrote after the battle that he did not like the ground: "It was certainly not proper for Highlanders." It was better suited for the Hanoverian style of fighting, not the Highland charge tactic of the Jacobites. Not everyone agreed, however. James Johnstone, a Jacobite officer, believed that the marshy ground was "well chosen for affording us a protection from the English cavalry".

THE LAST BATTLE

The Battle of Culloden on 16 April 1746 was the last major battle on British soil. At about 12.30 p.m., the Jacobites fired the first shot in an attempt to destroy the Hanoverians' cannons. The government soldiers fired back and smoke from the cannons blew towards the Jacobites, clouding their view. At 12.35 p.m., the Highland charge began, although the Jacobites had difficulty moving quickly over the boggy ground. The Jacobites broke through the Hanoverians' front line with hand-to-hand fighting, but lost 700 men in minutes. By 12.55 p.m., the Jacobites were surrounded. Five minutes later, they were in full retreat. The Duke of Cumberland ordered his cavalry to follow the fleeing Jacobites.

There was huge loss of life for the Jacobites, many of whom were weak with hunger and tired after marching all night. Over 1,000 Jacobites were killed compared with an official figure of 50 Hanoverians, although it was probably more.

Engraving of the Battle of Culloden

WEAPONS AND CLOTHING

The Jacobites carried less heavy weaponry than the Hanoverians, which is what allowed them to march so rapidly from Scotland to England and back again. They fought with broadswords and round wooden shields, although they also had muskets and cannons. The Hanoverians carried a Brown Bess musket and ammunition in a leather pouch. Hanoverian soldiers wore red coats (and were known as Redcoats). Jacobites wore tartan representative of their clan.

A Jacobite soldier

A Hanoverian soldier

CHAPTER 7 AFTER CULLODEN

Lord George Murray had gathered forces ready to fight on after the Culloden defeat, but Charles had had enough. Two days after the battle, he told the Jacobites to save themselves. He had no money with which to pay the men, and he knew that news of such a heavy defeat would reach the French. There would be no French invasion now.

Not all the Jacobites wanted to stop fighting, however. The Duke of Cumberland had offered an amnesty, but some clan chiefs kept fighting. The result was houses burned, livestock destroyed and people killed.

The Disarming Act of 1746 helped to break Highland culture by outlawing the wearing of tartan and the owning of weapons. The Hanoverians did not distinguish between clans who fought for them or against them. In fact, more Scots, including Highlanders, fought for the Hanoverians than the Jacobites in the 1745 Rebellion. About 80 Jacobites were executed and over 1,000 banished from Britain.

BONNIE PRINCE CHARLIE'S ESCAPE

After Culloden, Charles was a wanted man. He had escaped the battlefield with two of his closest officers, Felix O'Neill and John O'Sullivan. They had gone west to the Hebrides and Charles spent five months hiding from Cumberland's men around Scotland, being passed from one Jacobite supporter to another. At one stage, he dressed as a maid – called Betty Burke – and accompanied a lady called Flora Macdonald to the Isle of Skye. On 20 September 1746, Charles was finally able to leave Scotland and sail to France on the *Le Prince de Conti*.

After his defeat at Culloden, Bonnie Prince Charlie went into hiding in the Highlands.

WHAT HAPPENED NEXT

Charles spent the remaining years of his life in Italy, dying in 1789. His brother, Henry, was the last of the Stuarts. He died in 1807. The House of Hanover ruled Britain until 1901, when Queen Victoria died. England, Scotland and Wales remain largely Protestant countries. Northern Ireland is Protestant, while Ireland is still mainly Catholic.

INDEX

GLOSSARY

AMNESTY—pardon for offences made against the government or monarchy

BAYONET—knife designed to fit onto the end of a musket or other gun

CATHOLIC—Christian who is a member of the Roman Catholic Church, led by the Pope

CAVALRY—soldiers who fought on horseback

COMMANDER—person in control of armed troops

HANOVERIAN—person who worked for or supported the House of Hanover, led by George I and George II

HEIR—someone who will take over the responsibilities or titles of another person on their death, such as an heir to the throne who will take over as monarch from a previous king or queen

HIGHLANDER—person who lived in the Highlands of Scotland (roughly the northern areas of Scotland)

HIGHLAND CHARGE—type of fighting used by Highlanders in battle, where they would form into columns and charge at the enemy

LOWLANDER—person who lived in the Lowlands of Scotland (roughly the south and east of Scotland)

MASSACRE—event in which many people are deliberately killed

PROTESTANT—member of any of the Christian churches that broke away from the Roman Catholic Church during the 1500s

RECRUIT—person newly brought in to the armed forces

RISING—see **UPRISING**

SIEGE—blockade of a city in order to force the people living there to give up control of the city

STANDARD—flag representing a person or group of people

SUCCESSION—order of people who are next in line to the throne

TACTICS—way of organizing troops during battle

TORY—politician from the Tory political party. The party was traditionalist and believed in a monarch's right to rule. It was later associated with the Jacobites, although not all Tories were Jacobites.

TREATY—formal, documented, legally binding agreement

UPRISING—rebellion against the government

WHIG—politician from the Whig political party. The party believed in government by Parliament and a monarch. It supported the Hanoverians.

TIMELINE

1685

Feb: James II becomes King of England, Scotland and Ireland

1688

William of Orange invited to invade England

June: James II's son James Francis Edward Stuart is born

1688

Dec: James II escapes to France

1689

Glorious Revolution brings William and Mary to the throne

1689

27 July: Battle of Killiecrankie

1690

1 July: Battle of the Boyne

1714

1 Aug: Queen Anne dies; George of Hanover becomes king

1715

Jacobite Rebellion: the '15

13 Nov: Battle of Sheriffmuir

9–14 Nov: Battle of Preston

Dec: James Stuart arrives at Peterhead, north-east Scotland. Rebellion is already over.

1719

10 June: Battle of Glenshiel

1720

31 Dec: Charles Edward Stuart (Bonnie Prince Charlie) is born

1727

June: George II becomes king

1692

13 Feb: Glencoe massacre

1694

28 Dec: Queen Mary dies

1701

June: Act of Settlement

1702

8 Mar: William dies; Anne becomes queen

1707

May: Act of Union creates the United Kingdom of Great Britain, bringing together England, Wales and Scotland

1708

Jan: Failed attempt at French-backed rebellion

1745–46

Jacobite Rebellion: the '45

July: Charles Edward Stuart arrives in Scotland

21 Sep: Battle of Prestonpans

17 Jan: Battle of Falkirk

16 April: Battle of Culloden

SELECT BIBLIOGRAPHY

1715: The Great Jacobite Rebellion, Daniel Szechi (Yale University Press, 2006)

Battlefield Britain, Peter and Dan Snow (BBC Books, 2004)

BBC Website: "The Jacobite Cause" Louise Yeoman www.bbc.co.uk/history/british/civil_war_revolution/scotland_jacobites_01.shtml

Culloden Guidebook, Lyndsey Bowditch (The National Trust for Scotland, 2013)

Sweet William or The Butcher?, Jonathan Oates (Pen & Sword Military, 2008)

WEBSITES

www.educationscotland.gov.uk/scotlandhistory/jacobitesenlightenmentclearances/jacobiterisings/index.asp
Find out more about the Jacobites on this site.

http://www.parliament.uk/about/living-heritage/evolutionofparliament/legislativescrutiny/act-of-union-1707/
The background to the Act of Union and information about the Jacobite rebellions can be found on the official

PLACES TO VISIT

Culloden Battlefield Visitor Centre
Culloden Moor
Inverness
Highland IV2 5EU

www.nts.org.uk/Culloden/Home
Visit the site of the famous Battle of Culloden near Inverness and learn more at the visitor centre.

Palace of Holyroodhouse
Canongate
The Royal Mile
Edinburgh EH8 8DX

www.royalcollection.org.uk/visit/palace-of-holyroodhouse
Holyroodhouse became a royal palace during the reign of the Stuarts. Find out more about the Stuarts at a palace still used by monarchs today.